The Furies

VERSE PLAYS

William Considine

praise for 'the furies':

"At long last here's Bill Considine's considered, rollicking, breezy, deep, avant-post take on what Poetry is, what Theater is, and what happens when these arts tumble dance through history together only to land simultaneously on page and stage. Equal parts Sophocles and Ashbery, whose lineage from *Electra* right through to 'The Heroes' he invokes, Considine riffles the classics to fan a new breath of Pure Future. Perform these plays in your mind's eye or take the dare and produce them on stage – they are transportative. IOW, as Agamemnon says in 'Agamemnon, King of Cars', 'Let's prowl the great desert,/Whooping on speed,/In pick-up trucks or tanks./Let's all wear cowboy hats.'"

- Bob Holman

"The Furies is a terrific intervention, a unique contemporary dramatic verse collection with tropes of classic themes and characters. Considine has a poet's lyric ease, wit and calling, and a sensibility that travels through the complicated dynamics of history and war. As Orestes asks Electra, "Shall I talk of our childhood and/ all the times you silently/ stared at the summer leaves/ and tried to imagine, total death,/ nuclear war, all at once, and why?/ Do you remember our civil defense drills..." This is a refreshing "oral" book and generously available here for actors and poet-performers on the stage, as well as readers, in the hand. Bravo!"

- Anne Waldman

"Just when I was wondering whatever happened to poets' theater, along comes William Considine's thrilling collection of four verse plays, *The Furies*. Much poets' theater is heavy on the poetry (making it soporifically undramatic) or ignores language for quirky effects. Considine's work, however, is miraculous both onstage and in the ear. Not only that, he is learned, funny, witty, big-hearted, and timely. Take, for example, Solon's "daring disobedience" in 'Prologue: Prehistory': "You teach people / to say fantasies in public / and enjoy tall tales in meetings, / so faking will succeed / as the political intelligence / of our people." 'Lincoln in Queens' is as human as anything by Woody Guthrie, with a unique take on our most written-about president, who is "back from the dead in Queens," busy urging the narrator to "find the Furies" and speaking "of God like a lost lover: I lived in faith in the old-fashioned fable / of suffering and moral endurance. / We purged the blood-curse on our nation: / slavery! Now you can escape / the iron shackles of war, / the fable of blood atonement, / the faith of Furies." After small productions around New York City over many years, it's great to have these plays in one place to be read and reread, and, one hopes, performed again."

- Elinor Nauen

the operating system print//document

The Furies

ISBN 978-1-946031-09-9
Library of Congress Control Number 2017909510

copyright © 2017 by William Considine

edited and designed by Lynne DeSilva-Johnson
cover photo © 1983 by John E. Daniel
back cover photo © 1983 by Toyo Tsuchiya

is released under a Creative Commons CC-BY-NC-ND
(Attribution, Non Commercial, No Derivatives) License:
its reproduction is encouraged for those who otherwise could not afford its purchase in the case of academic, personal, and other creative usage from which no profit will accrue.   Complete rules and restrictions are available at:
http://creativecommons.org/licenses/by-nc-nd/3.0/

For additional questions regarding reproduction, quotation, or to request a pdf for review contact **operator@theoperatingsystem.org**

Professionals are hereby warned that professional production of these works is subject to a royalty. They are fully protected under the copyright laws. All rights, including professional, motion picture, recitation, public reading, radio broadcasting, television, video or sound taping, all other forms of mechanical or electronic reproduction, such as information storage and retrieval systems and photocopying, and rights of translation into foreign languages, are strictly reserved. Professional applications to produce in any such manner must additionally be made in advance to William Considine at considinew@gmail.com.

This text was set in Avenir Next, Dampfplatz, Minion, Franchise, and OCR-A Standard, printed and bound by Spencer Printing, in Honesdale, PA, in the USA. Books from The Operating System are distributed to the trade by SPD, with ePub and POD via Ingram.

the operating system
141 Spencer Street #203
Brooklyn, NY 11205
www.theoperatingsystem.org
operator@theoperatingsystem.org

The Furies

VERSE PLAYS

William Considine

for Emma

The Furies

PROLOGUE: PREHISTORY
AGAMEMNON, KING OF CARS
ELECTRA
LINCOLN IN QUEENS

Table of Contents

Prologue: Prehistory
13

Agamemnon, King of Cars
23

Electra
51

Lincoln In Queens
91

Poetics and Process
114

Archival Photos & Documents
117

Prologue: Prehistory

Prologue: Prehistory

had its first performance in May 1988,
in the Poets Theater Festival of the Poetry Project
at
St. Marks Church-in-the-Bowery, New York,
with the following cast:

Poet - James Honzik
Solon - Sparrow
Chorus - Mark Robbins, Philip Perkis

Directed by William Considine
Set by Deborah Gans

Poets Theater Festival directed by Bob Holman,
Alternate Direction by Elinor Nauen

CAST OF CHARACTERS

Poet
Solon
Chorus, of at least two persons

CHORUS and POET enter

POET
> I too will begin
> with signs of a beginning
> from long ago, in the Bronze Age
> of armored, shining Greeks.

POET withdraws to watch from stage left.

CHORUS
> Worn out by war and
> preparation for war,
> the people of Athens
> make all talk of war
> taboo taboo.
> The punishment for war cries
> is death.

CHORUS 2
> Swelling blood in the veins
> and heat of the young,
> a trader of olive oil
> and part-time poet named
> Solon rushes
> into the marketplace of Athens
> to act like a fool
> in a Persian helmet of straw,
> to chant a poem
> in the center of the city
> as a performance, urging war,
> in daring disobedience.

SOLON enters and takes center stage.

CHORUS 1
> Urging war as a madman
> immune from the laws:

SOLON
> War-weary people,
> where are our souls?
> We're buried alive
> with our ancestors
> and their forgotten gods,
> in graves on Salamis!
> Those spooky graves are ours!
> We must fight for our graves!

CHORUS 2
> His friends laugh and applaud.

CHORUS 1 and 2 clap in unison.

CHORUS 1
> Athens attacks the island Salamis.
> Solon serves as general.
> In a sharp fight, stabbing with spears,
> Athens captures the graves of Salamis.

CHORUS 2
> Solon rises to be the Law-Giver,
> leader of the city,
> out of his own wars.
> He makes laws on wooden plaques:

SOLON
> Law One: We forbid women
> to wear large pins in their gowns
> or hair, to disarm them
> as enemies of war,
> before they strike at our eyes.

Remember: in a raid
to the east, most of the men
of the expedition died,
stranded without food on an island
and cut down while hungry.

When the survivors returned in a few ships,
the women of Athens attacked them at the docks
with hair pins, in anger at the loss
of men on a raid.
Our few brave survivors so betrayed!
We must disarm the women.
No hairpins!
Law Two: We forbid women
to cry loudly and wail at funerals
for war dead. Tears are enough.
This wailing is foreign and
a political statement. It's come
with trading ships from Libya,
on the blue Afric shore.
Crying loudly is unpatriotic.

CHORUS 1
    Solon's wooden laws
    turn and fade in sun and rain.
    The city rages in civil war.
    Men who build temples prosper.
    Then comes an incident with hostages
    in the center of the city.

CHORUS 2
    Out of the blood-curse of Athens,
    the Tyrants take power.
    The History of the West begins.

POET steps in to lead the CHORUS as THESPIS.
CHORUS 1 and 2 move stage right
under the direction of POET.

CHORUS 1 AND 2
>One slow day in his old age,
>returned from exile,
>Solon walks down the Acropolis
>to watch the poet
>Thespis teach the sacred chorus
>his new concept:

POET
>- the tragic
>hymn and drama.

CHORUS 1 AND 2
>Solon the Law-Giver scolds
>at the birth of tragedy:

SOLON
>Your performance looks like
>law courts and city assemblies.
>You teach people
>to say fantasies in public
>and enjoy tall tales in meetings,
>so faking will succeed
>as the political intelligence
>of our people.

POET
>But Solon the Law-Giver,
>critic of free sorrow, is a fake
>madman, and a maker
>of myths to make war.

CHORUS 1 AND 2
>- a maker of
>myths to make war!

SOLON exits.

POET
> Theatre and theory
> are from the same source,
> meaning: to see
> the laws of life enacted.
> From that source, please,
> allow me to mix discourse,
> when words alone are so weak
> and surrendered to force.
> If a creative rush
> like a god allows one more
> inspiration and so life
> utterly given and fulfilled,
> and it can happen in one day
> poured into verses,
> let this be the evening
> late awakening to words.

𝕿𝖍𝖊 𝕰𝖓𝖉

Agamemnon, King of Cars

AGAMEMNON, KING OF CARS

First presented in a rehearsed reading in the New York Shakespeare Festival's Playwright's Unit at the Public Theater, in the Newman Theater, in November 1980, directed by John Nesci, with Andrew Callahan as Agamemnon, Eric Loeb as Meneleus, Ebbe Roe Smith as Odysseus, Diane Salinger as Iphigenia, and Charles McKenna, Rosemary Moore, Nancy Shinkle, Carol Kane, Terry Ann Bennett, Julie Ariola, Carla Howard, Joanne McEntire and Sherry Steiner in the Chorus.

Subsequently performed in a festival at Theater for the New City on June 5 and 6, 1982, directed by John Nesci, with Bill Sadler as Agamemnon, Matt Locricchio as Meneleus, Mike Moran as Odysseus, Mary Tepper as Iphigenia, and
Shelley Valfer, Len Jenkin, Dan Moran,
Charles McKenna, Rosemary Moore, Saun Ellis, Bridget Leicester, Joanne McEntire, Betty La Roe and Julie Ariola in the Chorus.

Music by Paul Galasso, set and tank by
John Arnone, costumes by Laura Drawbaugh, choreography by Pam Harling.

CAST OF CHARACTERS

Agamemnon
Meneleus
Odysseus
Iphigenia
Chorus of American citizens

SCENE

Bare Stage

CHORUS of several men in street clothes enter with a case of beer.
They put it down and casually stand around and sip beer.
MENELEUS in a business suit enters and addresses the audience

MENELEUS
And now - culture!
The Western world, foreseeing
Its own explosive ends, ceaselessly
Now thinks back upon itself,
To the origin of memory,
Back
To the enduring source of Western life,
Back
To the shape that still commands us,
Back
To the mighty king of Western men -
Agamemnon! King of Cars!

AGAMEMNON enters in modern clothes.
He carries a shield festooned with greasy auto parts and
emblazoned with a picture of a car or traffic jam. He carries a spear.

MENELEUS turns to the others.

Hey, everyone!
Agamemnon has an idea!

AGAMEMNON
This is great.
I, Agamemnon, have had a vision.
I say, let's cross the sea to the east
In ships and fight!

CHORUS OF MEN look at each other, puzzled, skeptical.

We must fight for the honor
Of Meneleus, my brother,
King of Busyness!

He always loved freedom like a wife
With automatic steering and lots
Of optional features.
But freedom was stolen from Busyness!
Yes! Fight and free the oil!

MENELEUS
Free the oil! While there's still some left!

CHORUS OF MEN *sip beer wearily, in unison.*

AGAMEMNON
Let's destroy all the great cities of the world!
Blast 'em! Smash 'em down!
Let's embrace the fate of men.
The chain of murder is the fate of men.
Progress is from war to world war to
World system now of Superwar!
The gods have given us nothing.
Let's call down the gods and kill them.
Bring forth the great catastrophe.
Armageddon is up to us.
This damned world must end.
End all that is unhonored.
Apocalypse will be quite a trip.
Boom! Boom! Wow! Bam!

MENELEUS
Agamemnon meant to say that
Always all the armor
Has broken the back of sturdy-limbed men
With the weight of many dead,
And now everywhere armor is piled,
So we must make more missiles and tanks
And ready our hearts for wild war,
Though the effort sickens us.

AGAMEMNON
>It's waiting that sickens us.
>Set your energy free!
>Between the dark sea and the walled city
>Waits the fate of heroes, the field of force.
>Let your blood flow with the universal
>Field of force.

CHORUS OF MEN
>All engines groan like the needy. The vast
>Train is on schedule and heavy with
>Grim projects. Refugees watch the cash
>Machines from silver Cadillacs. Startled
>Workmen bark out raw product. In air throb
>The charged products pleading. Sullen echoes
>Cry the possessed. Winter breaks with rain like
>Wires and the incessant drums of advent.

AGAMEMNON
>Let's prowl the great desert,
>Whooping on speed,
>In pick-up trucks or tanks.
>Let's all wear cowboy hats.

MAN TWO
>Why?

AGAMEMNON
>Because!

MAN TWO
>Why?

AGAMEMNON
>Because!

MAN TWO
>Why because?

AGAMEMNON
> Because! When we win Superwar,
> We'll be more famous than huge Roosevelt
> Or any of our fathers, fighters all
> And the smashers of Nazis and fascists!

MAN ONE
> Agamemnon is king!

MAN TWO
> No way! Wait a minute!
> We don't have a king.

AGAMEMNON
> I, Agamemnon, am king
> Of oil and the trade routes
> And king of cars.

MAN ONE
> Agamemnon is king of cars!
> Big-bodied, roaring cars that swarm
> In the streets nervously.

AGAMEMNON
> Give that man some money.

MENELEUS
> I think the public trend is toward his way
> Of thinking.

MENELEUS gives MAN ONE some money.

AGAMEMNON
> And the king of cars must take charge,
> In times of crisis and war,
> As the king of men.

MAN ONE
> Agamemnon is king
> Now of all the Americans!

MENELEUS
> And you've been drafted, Achilles.

MAN TWO
> My name is not Achilles.

MENELEUS
> Soon it will be, if you're good.
> Ajax. Our enemies will scream your names.

MENELEUS
> Sign here. "Achilles."
> It's just an image. Sign.
> Nothing is real.

MAN THREE
> I'd rather sign with the king of records
> And tapes.

AGAMEMNON
> The future's in cement.

MAN TWO
> I don't see the need for Superwar.

MENELEUS
> No jobs. The future's in cement.
> Let's all mix in and make cement,
> For missile silos and parking lots for tanks.
> Let's make missiles and tanks and drink hard
> And puke and fight and die, like men.

MAN THREE
> Hey, what about women?

MENELEUS
> You know how women are.

AGAMEMNON
> Women can stay home and make cement.

MENELEUS
> Okay! Let's get busy! Let's go!
> Taxes now, to defend you in Superwar!
> We'll make it up to you -
> We'll cut all public services.

MENELEUS takes money from the CHORUS OF MEN.
MENELEUS passes weird, complicated weapons to them.

> This one's broken.

MAN ONE
> How does this work?

MENELEUS
> You were educated at taxpayers' expense.
> You figure it out.

MAN TWO
> Hey, I think it's broken. When do soldiers get paid?

MENELEUS
> Sorry. We spent all we had on weapons.

AGAMEMNON
> Hurry with the laser-tank.

MENELEUS
> It doesn't work.

AGAMEMNON
	Then make more!

MENELEUS
	Speed it up! Let's go! Let's go!

MAN TWO
	You call this defense?
	Let's hear what Odysseus thinks.

AGAMEMNON
	Bah!

MAN THREE
	Odysseus will have a better plan.

MENELEUS
	Odysseus is washed-up. He's lost.
	He's on some personal trip.

MAN TWO
	Odysseus is still laughing
	And crafty. What does he think?

MENELEUS
	Who cares? The trend is
	Totally away from lost Odysseus.
	Soon we must cross the sea in ships and fight.

AGAMEMNON
	Superwar One is the war
	That will be won by winners!

MAN THREE
	Draft women! I'm not going abroad without girls.

MENELEUS
>   Soon you won't need women.
>   You'll have a laser-tank.

AGAMEMNON
>   Let's march down to the sea and ships!
>   Let's go!

CHORUS OF MEN whirls away from AGAMEMNON.
They walk to the rear, where they drink angrily and mutter.

AGAMEMNON
>   The war winds won't rise.

MENELEUS
>   They're so apathetic.

AGAMEMNON
>   Okay, we tried.
>   Let's give up and go home.
>   Or move to New Zealand.

MENELEUS
>   Never relent. See your wild dreams happen.
>   See, their tension and anger builds toward war.

MAN THREE
>   We've been sold some shoddy goods.
>   Give us our money back.

MENELEUS
>   I earned that money.

CHORUS OF MEN
>   Give us our money back!

MENELEUS
>   Alright, we'll compromise.

MENELEUS whispers to AGAMEMNON.

AGAMEMNON
    Alright, we'll compromise.
    We'll draft all the men.
    We'll draft Odysseus!
    That's the kind of symbol that wins Superwars!

MAN TWO
    Let's hear from Odysseus!

MAN THREE
    Let's hear from the women!

AGAMEMNON
    Let's go draft Odysseus!

CHORUS OF MEN follows AGAMEMNON toward stage right.

MAN ONE
    Can you lend me a dollar?

*In from stage right swirl WOMEN and MEN dancing,
including ODYSSEUS. CHORUS OF MEN joins the dancing.
Lights brighten high. Music.
This entire group is the full CHORUS.*

CHORAL INTERLUDE

*The men and women dance, first to the music
and the chant of MENELEUS and then to their song.
They become somewhat puzzled by the lyric to which they dance*

MENELEUS
    Okay, everyone!
    Let's draft all the men!
    Sing along!
    Let's draft all the men!

>   Let's draft all the men!
>   Come on!
>   Let's draft all the men!
>   Let's draft all the men!

CHORUS OF WOMEN *(singing)*
>   The king of cars has had a dream.
>   Drink, forget what freedom seemed.
>   Trash is all the world can be,
>   And trash, my dear, is never free.

The music and dance continue while WOMAN ONE speaks.

WOMAN ONE
>   We've been worn out and drugged out and bummed out,
>   But still these always young Americans
>   Flow forward, dancing and wild for freedom:
>   Teeming, registered Democrats, lovers
>   Of mankind, the people without leaders;
>   The sturdy few republicans,
>   Calling on the old republic or
>   Reveling in the glitter of old ores;
>   And all are Independents,
>   Distrusting all parties and politics;
>   Brave people! Too bad we've no ideas but cars.

The music and dance end.

AGAMEMNON
>   Look at them! Hey, let's take the women, too.
>   Draft them.

MENELEUS
>   We can't draft women.
>   Because women won't stand for it.

AGAMEMNON
>   But they'll let the men go?

MENELEUS
> Sure. You know how women are.

MENELEUS
> Odysseus!

ODYSSEUS
> Hey, it's the famous brother act!
> The sons of Atreus.
> How are you guys doing?

MENELEUS
> Pretty good.
> Agamemnon is the king of cars now,
> And I'm the king of busyness.

ODYSSEUS
> That doesn't even keep you off the streets.

AGAMEMNON
> And we have to draft you, Odysseus,
> As always.

MAN TWO
> They want us to cross the sea in ships
> And fight for the honor of Meneleus.

ODYSSEUS
> You can't draft me.
> I'm deranged. Whacko. Totally 4F.
> I have too much energy, in my chest and legs,
> And I have dreams that keep me awake.

MENELEUS
> Great Agamemnon is our leader
> And the lord of cars and trade routes,
> Oil and men, and he has dreams

> That the world must end in terror, fire,
> Screaming and glory, and we must obey.

ODYSSEUS
> Agamemnon is too late.
> His world has already ended.

AGAMEMNON
> Look again.

ODYSSEUS
> This life ceaselessly changes
> And changes now awesomely,
> In quiet and ease.
> Already the world has ended,
> Peacefully, and a new world has begun.
> From tensions and shocks,
> The long chain of murders has snapped.
> The chain of war lies broken in the dust.

AGAMEMNON
> Look again, madman.
> He is insane.
> We'll go without him.

AGAMEMNON turns to go.

ODYSSEUS
> Hear me out! I've become an oracle!

MENELEUS
> A what?

ODYSSEUS
> I've gone into the oracle business.

MENELEUS
> Fairly whacko.

ODYSSEUS
    And I announce -

AGAMEMNON
    So what?

WOMAN TWO
    Let's hear Odysseus!

ODYSSEUS
    Thank you. I announce -
    That centuries of war have smashed the fates
    And all their gloomy towers and walls.
    The cities stand without walls.
    The people stand open to the heavens.
    The old fates are exhausted.
    Paranoia got so sick it died.
    The war-state has died and gone to heaven.
    The war machine has run out of gas.

MENELEUS
    There's plenty of oil in outer space.

WOMAN TWO
    Tell us your plan, if you have one.

ODYSSEUS
    We must rewrite the laws of physics.
    The universe is not a field of force.
    Force is the empty word of Agamemnon.
    The cosmos is a field of play.
    The world dances, to rock and roll.
    Rock and roll is the motion of love.
    People dance and play much more than they fight.
    These are well-known facts.

WOMAN TWO
    What's your plan?

ODYSSEUS
    You tell me.

WOMAN TWO
    Get serious about disarmament!

CHORUS
    Hooray!

MAN TWO
    Or else nuclear weapons will kill us!

AGAMEMNON
    Here comes the laser-tank! Look!
    How big it is!

ALL look to the laser-tank, pushed slowly onstage.
AGAMEMNON stabs ODYSSEUS with his spear and kills him.

    Look! Odysseus killed himself.
    Unhappy man, insomniac dreamer!
    And a really nice person, too.

CHORUS
    No!

AGAMEMNON
    But unrealistic.
    He played with the fates.
    The chain of murder is the fate of men.
    It coiled and broke Odysseus.

CHORUS
    No!

AGAMEMNON
    Let the utterance of great Odysseus
    Inspire us now in Superwar,

To end this world of war! Men!

CHORUS OF WOMEN
    No!

AGAMEMNON
    Let the laws forbid women
    To scream at the funerals of war,
    Shrill and unpleasant.
    They can scream at their husbands,
    Absent or at home and weep,
    If that's their nature.

MENELEUS
    We can win without Odysseus.

AGAMEMNON
    He slowed us down with wild ideas.
    His thoughts are for the future.
    Here, help with the laser-tank.
    We're losing time.

Several discouraged people push the tank.

WOMAN THREE
    This tank is made of cement.

MENELEUS
    It grips the road better.

WOMAN FOUR
    Is this the MX missile or the XM tank?

MENELEUS
    Both. We combined them, to save time
    And use more concrete.
    X, the unknown, has replaced the cross.
    M, as always, is for money and might.

MAN ONE
> It's broken.

AGAMEMNON
> Let's go, men! We'll fix it.
> Me first, remember, and then you, Ajax.
> Here's a nuclear weapon.
> Just pull the pin and throw it.

AGAMEMNON gives a heavy bomb to MAN TWO.

MAN TWO
> It's made of cement!

AGAMEMNON
> Let's go, let's win, let's go!

CHORUS stirs sluggishly.

WOMAN THREE
> Wait! You can't take all the men.

MENELEUS
> Hey, sister, you don't like men anyway, right?

WOMAN THREE
> Wrong!

MAN THREE
> I think we'd win if we took the women.
> No one in his right mind would shoot
> A young woman.

AGAMEMNON
> For discipline, we must separate the sexes.
> They weren't getting along, anyway.

MANY
> Says who?

MENELEUS
> And we're giving everyone a divorce
> Now, to save fuss later.

WOMAN FOUR
> We'll settle our own differences, thanks.

MENELEUS
> Look, you women libbers wanted jobs.
> Now you've got all the jobs.

AGAMEMNON
> A woman's place is in the tank shop.

WOMAN ONE
> This is not what I wanted.

CHORUS fidgets grimly.

AGAMEMNON
> Where is the spirit of Superwar?

MAN TWO
> It died with the fascists.

MENELEUS takes AGAMEMNON aside.

AGAMEMNON
> They won't do what I tell them.

MENELEUS
> Don't worry, don't think, don't plan.
> Let money wreak its will.
> Trust only to money, and all else will die.
> Superwar will come.

WOMAN FIVE
> We don't really have a king.
> We're still free to do our thing.

WOMAN SIX
> We could work the earth in peace,
> If we use our elbow-grease.

AGAMEMNON
> What do I do?

MENELEUS
> Brother!
> I've had a vision!
> I can't believe it.

AGAMEMNON
> What?

MENELEUS
> Maybe I read it in a book.

AGAMEMNON
> What?

MENELEUS
> You, great lord of men,
> Must kill your daughter, Iphigenia.
> You must slash her bare heart on the altar
> With a long knife and stuff her heart
> With a handful of dollars.
> And then the winds will favor war.

AGAMEMNON
> I don't think I have a daughter.

MENELEUS
> It's the best I can do.

AGAMEMNON
Iphigenia? Iphigenia?

WOMAN FOUR
There's no one here by that name.

AGAMEMNON (to WOMAN FIVE)
You can be Iphigenia, tragic
And immortal at my altar.

WOMAN FIVE
That's no altar. That's a cement tank.
I'm not going.

AGAMEMNON (to IPHIGENIA)
You! You can be the sacrifice!

IPHIGENIA - that is, WOMAN SEVEN -
steps forward slowly and gravely.

IPHIGENIA
Now comes the high pity of tragic
Recognition.

WOMAN SIX
I thought she might.

IPHIGENIA
Someone must know that she is Iphigenia,
And know that she must die on the altar
Of nations, and dying, she must bless
The war-state that ennobles her blood.

IPHIGENIA walks slowly to the tank.
She pulls out a knife.

AGAMEMNON
Oh, no. She's gonna do it.

MENELEUS
Do the job.

IPHIGENIA climbs onto the tank as altar.

IPHIGENIA
Anything for drama!
Maybe dead I can get parts
As murdered women in all the new movies.
Is my agent here? Kill me!

WOMAN SIX
I've already seen this movie!

CHORUS
We've already seen this movie!

IPHIGENIA, on the tank that is her altar,
holds her knife above her.

IPHIGENIA
Sing, if you will, after the hours of
Prayer and honor the stranger
Gods who march late and pound through
The kitchens. Their daughters too name the
Ancients. They are bathed with flute girls
For the late banquet. They too know sacrifice

And the offerings of words in waves
Before dinner: Almighty the iron sprawl
And the ores washed in tears, gold and
Fragrant oils. Stand the condemned in a field
Of names and grant them a release,
To dance in their homes with abandon.
With product and the right wires pulled,
Their hard new voices use the radio.

IPHIGENIA throws down her knife.

The war winds won't rise! The gods forbid war!

WOMAN THREE
The war winds won't rise!

WOMAN FOUR
The gods forbid war!

WOMAN TWO
The king of cars is not the lord of Americans!

CHORUS
Hooray!

> *ODYSSEUS leaps up.*
> *He takes the spear and shield from*
> *AGAMEMNON and throws them aside.*

MAN ONE
Odysseus!

WOMAN ONE
You were dead.

ODYSSEUS
Like I said - everything is play!
Not quite! It was horrible!

CHORUS
What's it like, when you're dead?

ODYSSEUS
I went to hell and felt too much, awful,
too hard, too fast. All of history was there.
I lived with the ghosts.
Everyone circled, mumbling blood.
I found Achilles, who was sad
and said death is very boring,

> Just memories, on and on, the same thing
> And now with no hope of redemption.
> He said to live simply
> And never go off to war. This from Achilles!
> I thought hard too, and painfully.
> Our time is urgent and maybe too late.
> The new words, that overthrow the rule
> Of force, will take so long
> To understand, but they are
> Already among us,
> Drawn into life to face the new terrors.
> All we can do
> Is keep the peace in our generation,
> And so give ourselves into the future
> And so raise history out of hell
> And see this in our lives.

IPHIGENIA gets off the tank and rejoins the others.

WOMAN SIX
> What do we do with Agamemnon?

ODYSSEUS
> Send him home with unbloodied hands.

AGAMEMNON
> If I go home a loser,
> Clytemnestra will kill me.

ODYSSEUS
> No! You'll find peace.
> The chain of murder is broken.

WOMAN FIVE
> Odysseus is not the heir of Agamemnon.
> We will all decide.

WOMAN ONE
> We are all the heirs of the gods
> And bless a new world.

MENELEUS
> I'll get right to work.

AGAMEMNON
> I'm sorry. Smashing the world
> Was just a bad dream I had. Forget it.

MAN ONE
> We have energy enough for a lifetime,
> Each of us, in every limb.

> *AGAMEMNON and MENELEUS fade away*
> *by exiting backward, waving good-bye.*
> *ODYSSEUS waves to them.*

ODYSSEUS (singing)
Dead powers cry from their graves!
Too bad for them, tra la!

IPHIGENIA (singing)
The future's ours! We can be saved!
Hooray for life!

CHORUS (singing)
Tra la!

> *CHORUS dances.*

- The End -

Electra

ELECTRA

An excerpt from *Electra* had a staged reading at The Ritz, an art exhibit by Artists Collaborative (Colab) in Washington D.C. in April 1983, with Ilona Granet as Electra.

Its first performance was at the Terminal, an art exhibit in the former Brooklyn Army Terminal, New York City in October 1983, with the following cast:

Electra - Sharon Take
Chorus - Marjorie Ohle
Clytemnestra - Susan Riskin
Orestes - David Stocker

Painted set - John Shaw
Stage furniture - Frank Shifreen
Lighting - Michael Curtin
Stage Manager - Marjorie Ohle
Assistant Stage Manager - Dave Lancet

Directed by Kevin O'Brien
Produced by William Considine

A video by Franz Vila of the performance, entitled *Electra: The Furies*, with music by Christian Marclay, was first shown at the Red Bar and on a Manhattan Cable Television public access channel in January 1984.

CAST OF CHARACTERS

Electra
Clytemnestra
Orestes
Chorus

SCENE

The tomb of the warlord Agamemnon

The tomb of the warlord Agamemnon. ELECTRA is onstage

ELECTRA
>The tragic cycle turns,
>turns faster, dizzy to
>destroy!
>It's down to us, the terrified,
>in our generation, now,
>in our moral life to
>destroy war!
>For me, the charge is total.
>Agamemnon! Warlord
>of the West! Father!
>I am Electra!
>I'm stuck at your tomb.
>I'm here to pray for you,
>to you.
>They will not let us rest
>in peace.
>Settle in the earth,
>be stone forever.
>Let your war-spirit go,
>out of this tomb and gone.
>Let the new world
>blossom with spring, ending
>one more winter.
>You were the great destroyer
>of cities. Help me
>destroy war!
>I'm powerless now!
>It's too much, too late.
>Hope is impossible!

CHORUS enters.

CHORUS
>Don't cry, Electra!
>It breaks my heart.

ELECTRA
>   These males lusting
>   war go boom, the big boss
>   apes strutting air of command
>   with big bucks for
>   their iron warheads,
>   they'll kill us in
>   Bible-ending glory!

CHORUS
>   Cool out, right? Stay cool.
>   Since the storming
>   of Europe and the bombs
>   that shook Asia,
>   everything is cold
>   on the brink,
>   but still it's shock-time, right,
>   to work hard calmly for peace.

ELECTRA
>   How many wars could you watch
>   last night on television?
>   The tanks and bombs, the refugees,
>   massacres, blasts, the dead, our world!

CHORUS
>   Use your body's indifference
>   and appetites,
>   use the sunshine's indifference,
>   go on, work for peace!

ELECTRA
>   Don't we all?

CHORUS
>   But you ask too much,
>   you make life impossible!

ELECTRA
> So much has to change!

CHORUS
> A woman governs the earth now.

ELECTRA
> Ah, Clytemnestra!

CHORUS
> Maybe
> we'll persuade her gently,
> in time. You most of all
> can help her change.

ELECTRA
> Yes, because I'm her
> daughter. She hates me!

CHORUS
> You scare your mother
> with your visions.

ELECTRA
> All Clytemnestra
> knows is tragedy.
> Tragic fate is her noble mask.
> Her great beauty is a mask
> made of wonderful deaths.
> Tragic fate must die!
> I have to replace my mother.
> I know!
> It seems so sick, psychotic.

CHORUS
> It's a simple change,
> in beauty over the years.

ELECTRA
> We don't have years.
> You know it's too late.
> Don't you?

CHORUS
> I know, yes!
> All will die
> soon of the tensions.

ELECTRA
> I can't let that happen.
> I have to make time.

CHORUS
> I pray there's time.
> I pray for you.
> You're lost to the tensions.

ELECTRA
> Weep at the meaningless tomb.
> Politics as usual is doom.
> The only way to save mankind
> is to change the structure of our mind,
> too late, impossible, mad I know,
> but so flow
> the currents of an electrified soul.
> The moral life rides madness to its goal.

CHORUS
> Let's surrender our pride
> in genius visions God will chide
> and punish. Cry to the church
> to guide our desperate search.
> Only the past holds enough time
> to condemn the crime
> and evil sin: any order
> to war.

ELECTRA
> I'll take up anything at hand,
> God, love, a rock band,
> and tear at it like an ape
> sniffing for food in any shape,
> but they all break up.
> Take love. I didn't make up
> that rough emotion. I did take up
> its delusions. You wake with a cold eye
> and shallow breath,
> gasping in a world ordered in death
> wish, where love too has to die.

CHORUS
> Everything is this and yet
> that. Our Western culture
> circles the earth like a vulture,
> and its returning cycles set
> the stage for new life.
> Our ancient meanings fall apart.
> Their nonsense occupies the heart
> with signs of hope. Logic is a lie.
> Love takes parting as its wife.
> From dreams, we wake up
> into nightmares. Industries shake up
> our lives. Nothing is at hand. We try!
> We try! Our culture feeds on the vultures.

ELECTRA
> And so I wrap myself in solitude
> that deepens every day alone and silent.
> Ever more grim, more quiet, more sure,
> I sicken, age, current
> with the culture's death convulsions.
> I'm from a house of solitude,
> a family of madness, and I grow into it,
> neglected and poor, my fate,
> the daughter of the war-king,

> searching my place and culture in outcries.
> The fates have changed. All I know is
> my choice of a place at the iron tomb,
> and I give myself into the darkness
> that was given to me.

CHORUS
> You've closed into solitude,
> lost to us,
> and given into dangers,
> as you say, into madness.
> We have no hopes for you.
> Good luck! You make me nervous.
> You've always been cold,
> self-absorbed and driven.
> We like people who like
> to go to the movies with us
> and chat away the night.
> We don't have time to...

CLYTEMNESTRA enters.

CLYTEMNESTRA
> Today there are many
> fine films at popular prices.

ELECTRA
> You killed Agamemnon!

CLYTEMNESTRA
> The warlord had to die!

ELECTRA
> Home from the war came
> the smashers of fascists,
> to wrench iron from the
> earth into goods.

CLYTEMNESTRA
> But the blood stayed inside
> inside them and smelled
> like whiskey and vomit.

ELECTRA
> First you castrated him.
> It was always money,
> wasn't it, Mother? Money!

CLYTEMNESTRA
> Where was the fruit
> of the sacrifice?

ELECTRA
> On Sunday and at dusk,
> there were nice rides in the car.

CLYTEMNESTRA
> My washing machines
> filled a fallout shelter.
> How could I take the end?
> So much to be afraid of
> drew adrenalin.
> My thyroid swelled.
> In my neck
> I made energy.
> It filled even my eyes
> with the glare of
> suspicion.
> And there was a lot
> to suspect about the lord
> of men, Agamemnon.

CHORUS
> I don't ask about mysteries
> or which was the murder.

> I know the war machines
> groan with becoming more.
> Where is the peace
> that goes with the land?
> When's the big occasion?

ELECTRA
> The groans of the poor
> who have to live without
> jobs are the music
> she sells to
> hide her money supply,
> and that's in guns.
> Her blood money
> gives no ending to
> the death of Agamemnon.
> If she can think
> of more enormous war, I can
> think, "Pig for slaughter."
> Your neck on the line.
> Who will be the next to kill?
> Orestes will kill you first.

CLYTEMNESTRA
> I think she's hung herself.

ELECTRA
> Orestes is savage.
> He mates likes a bull.
> He hates women, because of
> what you did.
> You killed our father
> in a poisonous net of
> home presumptions,
> comforts at costs
> in the real world.
> You hacked off his head
> on the tile floor in

the bathroom, to seem
bigger than a poor man
and the heir of Agamemnon.

CHORUS
The warlord had to die.
He died, so forget it.

ELECTRA
Violence fills my head
with grim mouthings.
What will trigger peace?
All is corrupt,
distorting all love,
all cruel, all domination,
all distorted by
tensions of destruction.
All the world is in the
iron tomb of Agamemnon.

CLYTEMNESTRA
Get with it.
You're out of your time
and in personal financial trouble.
With your connections,
you could get a new job for a woman,
in a defense industry.
But no, you're a neurotic,
a disgrace. Not all the world
is in an iron tomb.
What a sadly revealing slogan.
This is just your father's tomb,
and he was a drunk.
We disagree about the way
to peace.
You think in totalities,
like the metaphysics of men.

> Transform yourself, take a lover,
> find peace in bed and at the table,
> in friends and children, like a woman.
> All you have to do is work with me.

ELECTRA
> I'll wait for Orestes.

CLYTEMNESTRA
> That's pretty old-fashioned,
> waiting for a man
> to topple your mother.

ELECTRA
> I wait in the rise of women
> the most likely source
> of basic change.

CLYTEMNESTRA
> Most new women accommodate,
> like most old men.

ELECTRA
> I can wait.

CLYTEMNESTRA
> I'll let Orestes kill me.
> If you hate me, I might
> as well be dead, except
> I won't let you
> control me like that.

ELECTRA
> I don't want him
> to kill you!
> Look, I agree!
> That angry Agamemnon
> killed my sister!

Iphigenia!
To make war!

CLYTEMNESTRA
>But Orestes will be
>forgiven for killing me.
>It's unfair.
>I'll change it. It's a myth.
>I'll kill the bastard.
>Aegisthus was my love
>and so the true father,
>not Agamemnon, that
>god-big pretender.
>Stop mourning the man.

ELECTRA
>Why mourn?
>The earth will shine on, blue
>with gray, slow, swirling mist
>in other heavens,
>the most beautiful planet,
>with or without our life.

CLYTEMNESTRA
>Life will go
>to the place where all
>the men have gone, where
>death together is more sacred
>than a good meal.
>That's where Aegisthus is gone,
>abandoning me, to save
>his own skin.
>And I'm to be the state sacrifice,
>killed by my son Orestes
>to make men the most?
>No way! The cub.
>I'll snuff him out.

>   Darling daughter, don't
>   say no all the way
>   to the end of my life.

ELECTRA
>   When you die,
>   the tragic cycle will end.
>   Orestes will be forgiven.
>   I know it's not fair.
>   But just you go, just you go.

CLYTEMNESTRA
>   This time the cycle will end
>   when I kill Orestes.
>   That will be peace at last.
>   If you don't love me,
>   you must kill me.
>   No more Orestes.
>   Do what you want or shut up.

CLYTEMNESTRA offers ELECTRA a knife.

ELECTRA
>   Make me the sacrifice,
>   so my cries might reach
>   through concrete cathedrals
>   to interrupt the civilized
>   party talk of creation.

CLYTEMNESTRA keeps the knife.

CLYTEMNESTRA
>   You're stronger than the giants,
>   who were buried by the gods.
>   And the gods have fled
>   my on-coming Furies,
>   who will haunt even Orestes
>   if I die.

CHORUS
> If the Furies get loose
> from deep in the earth,
> then will be vengeance
> on the gods in one
> night of terror.

MESSENGER enters.

MESSENGER
> Is this the ancient house of the warlord Atreus?

CHORUS
> It is.

MESSENGER
> At last! Is the queen here?
> Clytemnestra?

CLYTEMNESTRA
> I am Clytemnestra.

MESSENGER
> I have urgent news.
> To the point: Orestes is dead.

SILENCE.

CLYTEMNESTRA
> Who sent you?
> Who are you working for?

MESSENGER
> I promised Orestes
> I'd find you.

CLYTEMNESTRA
> What did he say?

MESSENGER
    Please wish him peace,
    as he wanted peace with you.
    These are his ashes.
    He was killed in Asia
    and with him many hopes
    burned in napalm.
    I've wandered the earth
    with his remains
    for years searching for the
    sky-lit house of Atreus.

MESSENGER places an urn at CLYTEMNESTRA'S feet.

CLYTEMNESTRA
    Is this Orestes?

MESSENGER
    I saw him die slowly
    in awful pain, bitter.
    His death was heroic.
    He bled a few quarts.

CLYTEMNESTRA
    Prove it's Orestes.

MESSENGER
    This is his ring, his father's ring,
    Agamemnon's ring.

MESSENGER gives ring to Clytemnestra.

ELECTRA
    Ashes!

MESSENGER
    We passed through here once,
    crossed these bridges to the sea

to be stationed abroad,
to hold the shattered center
of the West. Backwards in time,
he bled like men
on the barbed wire,
storming the shores of Europe
to break the fascists.
Backwards he bled like men
in no man's land
charging machine guns.
A war to end war!
He was torn apart like boys
in civil war
to end a form of slavery.
He was scalped, taking the land,
in desperate magic of the natives.
He froze in revolution
to free what? The new world!
He died as the generations of men die,
like flowers in the seasons,
in blood spill into
the earth of our breed.

CHORUS
So many millions died
fighting the fury
of tyrannies applied
in our century.

Hail them, the fighters!
They weren't victims.
Their souls are lighter
than our brooding hymns.

They spring from the earth
as each generation
gives way to birth
in regeneration,

with their return.
Undefeated, they return.

CLYTEMNESTRA
I've lost a son.
His name was an ax at my heart
and bitterly I'd lost my love.
It's easy to despair,
because our despair is close
to the facts and sees the outcome
even of our surges of enthusiasm.
So, let's despair.
As the gods fled, they left us
only their lingering in words
that call out of me now,
words like "pray,"
in confusion.
Pray my power
keeps the peace a while.
Leave us to mourn the fate
of our family, come back bloodless.
Build a tomb for Orestes.
We'll build many iron tombs
to cover the earth, prove our might
and remorseless will. We'll terrify
our enemies. Go! Build tombs!

ELECTRA
We've not given up
on life beyond terror.

CLYTEMNESTRA
Me too! Someday we'll see.
Meanwhile, there are jobs building tombs.
Go, build your tombs, and give
this messenger nothing,
to help him rely on himself.

For bringing such bad news,
he's lucky to live.

CHORUS
We're sorry with you
in more grief unearned by
the royal mother.

CLYTEMENSTRA
Yes, thank you.

CHORUS
The death of the son
can mean the end
of the tragic cycle.
Wasn't that the promise
that was called the Redemption?

CHORUS and MESSENGER exit.

ELECTRA
Do you remember much about Orestes?

CLYTEMNESTRA
That damn nurse
stole him from me!
She didn't trust me
and my faith in the man
Aegisthus. Orestes grew up
somewhere else and died.
And foreigners and the gods
too spoke evil of me to the boy.

ELECTRA
Maybe he'll rise from the dead.
Don't these feel like the days
of the dreadful judgment?

CLYTEMNESTRA opens the door of the tomb.

CLYTEMNESTRA
    The myths are dead.
    Dead is complete, dead.
    Even the word of Jesus
    did what, finally?
    Change the phrases and forms
    of prayer? Even the word of
    Jesus couldn't begin
    to end war in two thousand years.

ELECTRA
    You don't really believe
    terror will keep peace.

CLYTEMNESTRA
    I believe in my breakfast.
    I make warheads for war.
    There will be a war,
    disease, starvation, bugs,
    locusts! Grab what you can
    in this life. Eat up.
    Won't you come have
    dinner with me?

ELECTRA
    What are you doing?

CLYTEMNESTRA
    From now on,
    I'll live in the iron tomb.
    Soon we'll all live in iron
    tombs. It'll be nice in there.
    We can mourn the loss of our love,
    in private.

ELECTRA
    Mother, I'm afraid.

CLYTEMNESTRA
    Then take my hand.

ELECTRA
    I won't go in there!

CLYTEMNESTRA
    Then you'll keep your nightmares alone.

ELECTRA
    You make those nightmares!

CLYTEMNESTRA
    Come to me for comfort.
    I want you to.
    I'll keep the door open.

ELECTRA
    Close it! Let me be!

CLYTEMNESTRA
    You can mourn a while for Orestes.
    Then there's no more mourning
    outside my home, where our enemies
    can see, only within, with me.

>   *CLYTEMNESTRA exists, center, into the tomb.*
>   *She closes the heavy doors.*
>   *ELECTRA is alone onstage with the urn.*

ELECTRA
    Orestes is dead!
    And all my hopes for his return!
    I'll fulfill the myth myself, then,
    and make the new, the just order,
    somehow.

>Now my time of tears must die.
>Who am I now, if not the woman mourning?
>I am the woman mourning!
>Electra. Abandon the name now.
>Hard to outgrow so much of me.
>Electra, modern, the pulse of the force field.
>Electra, the synapse snap at the nerves,
>the sterile mother of protons, neutrons,
>photons, electrons, the strong force, charm,
>dark matter, accelerating,
>attraction and repulsion, power,
>power lines, power plants, current, flow,
>boiling water, radioactive core,
>fission, fusion, warhead, critical mass,
>chain reaction, fire blast, shock war:
>Electra is released!

MESSENGER enters.

MESSENGER
> Electra?

ELECTRA
> No, no more. Electra's gone.

MESSENGER
> I want to see her.

ELECTRA
> She's vaporized, an ion.
> You can't see her.
> What she had of herself was old
> names, roles. She stripped them away -
> just an orbit of feelings
> and cloud chamber tracings.

MESSENGER
> Is she alive?

ELECTRA
> She was out of her time
> and disintegrated under great pressures.

MESSENGER
> Is she alive?

ELECTRA
> She's every living thing.
> She's the wave and particle
> of everything. Can you feel her tensions?

MESSENGER
> Is Electra dead?

ELECTRA
> Even the living are nearly dead.

MESSENGER
> Who are you? You scorn
> questions of life and death.

ELECTRA
> Electra's dead.
> She called it release.

MESSENGER
> Who are you? You hold
> the ashes of Orestes.

ELECTRA
> I'm the keeper of dead spirits,
> and I'm the dead man's sister.

MESSENGER
> Iphigenia? Is it you?

ELECTRA
> She's in Hollywood.
> Please let me alone.
> My brother's dead.

MESSENGER
> If you're a sister
> of Orestes, I must talk with you.
> I've carried his ashes
> for years, wandering.

ELECTRA
> Thank you! Forgive me.
> In so much loss, I win at little games.
> In so little meaning, I hide in words.

MESSENGER
> I have to give the last words
> of Orestes to Electra.

ELECTRA
> Then Electra's alive. Broken or growing,
> what does it matter, I'm Electra.

MESSENGER
> You're Electra?

ELECTRA
> Yes.

MESSENGER
> How can I know?

ELECTRA
> Everyone knows I'm Electra.
> Ask anyone.

MESSENGER
    I can't ask anyone.
    I need to talk with you in private.

ELECTRA
    I'm anxious to hear
    the last words of Orestes.

MESSENGER
    Orestes has not yet had the last word.

ELECTRA
    And will his ghost walk?
    Will it march for peace?

MESSENGER
    As I cry out for peace, so will Orestes.

ELECTRA
    Don't let mystic talk diminish his death.

MESSENGER
    Orestes is alive.

ELECTRA
    Where?

MESSENGER
    I am Orestes.

ELECTRA
    You? Are you Orestes?

MESSENGER (ORESTES)
    Can you be Electra? What joy!

ELECTRA and ORESTES embrace.

ELECTRA
> Yes, it's perfect! I'm holding you!

ORESTES
> I see you, hold you, hear you!

ELECTRA
> But are you Orestes?
> Why'd you lie? Why'd
> you say you were dead?

ORESTES
> If Clytemnestra knows
> I've come back,
> she'll have me murdered.

ELECTRA
> She killed our father.

ORESTES
> I didn't come for revenge.

ELECTRA
> Then why are you here?
> Prove you're Orestes.

ORESTES
> Shall I talk of our childhood and
> all the times you silently
> stared at the summer leaves
> and tried to imagine, total death,
> nuclear war, all at once, and why?
> Do you remember our civil defense drills,
> down to the school basement in lines?
> Do you remember the air raid siren,
> tested every Monday at eleven a.m.,
> from the roof of the firehouse,
> and the strange meaning imagined

all the time in airplanes overhead,
total death, nuclear war, and why?
And the radio: "Beeeee...
Had this been an actual alert..."

ELECTRA
"You would have been instructed..."

ORSTES
"To turn your dial to 740..."

ELECTRA
"Or 1240 kilowatts for further
instructions!" It is you!

ORESTES
And we have to be quiet
and plan. We must act
now, no delay.

ELECTRA
Clytemnestra!

ORESTES
Killing won't end killing.
Laying down arms
will change the truth.
It will break
the spell of blood.

ELECTRA
Did a god speak to you?

ORESTES
In a broken grove
across a river far from here,
in my strange awakening
everything was stone

        making steel.
        Statues commanded me
        in red gleam of unholy
        night fires and clangor of the vast
        old mills along the river
        making danger.
        But it was the dawn!
        And the sun-god Apollo
        said to me calmly,
        "You have obeyed the gods
        too long for our love.
        Now you must be punished
        with our last commandment:
        Make peace."
        And I decided to give up to
        Clytemnestra this knife
        with which the fates would
        have me kill her.

ORESTES shows ELECTRA the knife.

    ELECTRA
        She's closed in the tomb
        and speaks of the Furies.
        She swears she'll snuff
        you out, kill you!

    ORESTES
        Then I will be
        the sacrifice of change.

    ELECTRA
        We don't need martyrs.
        Listen to me:
        there isn't much blood.
        Too many must be torn
        in the dumb search for
        appeasement of blood talk.

ORESTES
> I'm the son of Agamemnon.
> These have become my days.
> I am prepared to die.
> We have to act now.
> Clytemnestra has to suspect me.

ELECTRA
> Agamemnon had just stepped
> into a bath from a journey
> of a thousand miles home,
> when she tapped on the door
> and stepped in to kill him.

ORESTES
> Call in the people,
> to do more than witness
> the risk of peace,
> to share in it.

ELECTRA
> May the future believe
> in prevailing over
> the murder madness, as it will.
> Let's begin the change.

ORESTES
> I'll surrender the knife
> in front of the people.

ELECTRA
> And I'll beg forgiveness
> for all my threats.

ELECTRA calls offstage.

> Orestes is here, alive!
> He calls to the tomb, to
> Clytemnestra. Orestes
> offers peace!

ORESTES
> This reeks of incest taboo
> and sleazy theories.
> Why do I always talk
> of the good and peace?
> Those are delusions of the weak,
> that disable their lives.
> People are brutal, stupid.
> Peace is prim talk of losers.
> Down into darkest daydreams
> of glory and world domination,
> no less, sinks my brain,
> just a twist of the chains
> of pornographic domination
> masked with good words to whip
> all outcries into meanings,
> torture my pain into peace,
> my kingdom of release.

CLYTEMNESTRA enters from the tomb.
CHORUS enters.

CLYTEMNESTRA
> Stranger, do you have another message,
> or do those wild eyes mean treachery?

ORESTES
> I'm not a stranger anymore.
> I'm your son Orestes.

CLYTEMNESTRA
> I see that now.

ORESTES
> I haven't come to kill you.

CLYTEMNESTRA
> I won't let you kill me.

ORESTES
> I don't want to kill you.
> Mother, I've returned.

CLYTEMNESTRA
> Just don't come closer.

ORESTES
> I'm glad to see you.

CLYTEMNESTRA
> You lied. You said to
> my face you were dead.

ORESTES
> I was afraid of the fear
> of the old fates of murder.

CLYTEMNESTRA
> Be afraid of them still.
> I am.

ORESTES
> What died was the myth
> of Orestes
> the princely killer.
> All meaning changes.
> Look around you.

CLYTEMNESTRA
> Dreamers have talked before.

ORESTES
> Their talk accelerates
> into new meanings.

CLYTEMNESTRA
> Only in the depths of dreams.

ORESTES
>	From Apollo, I got
>	the vision to see
>	through the spell
>	of our house of warlords.

CLYTEMNESTRA
>	My power is more than a spell.

ORESTES
>	Your spell has to go into the past.

CLYTEMNESTRA
>	You did, you came to take
>	my power, you bastard.

ORESTES
>	I came to give up the knife of
>	the on-going revenge.

CLYTEMNESTRA
>	Did Apollo promise
>	you victory?

ORESTES
>	He promised me hardships
>	in an old-fashioned fable
>	of pain and moral endurance.
>	I gave you the ashes
>	of the old Orestes.

ELECTRA
>	I won't threaten you
>	anymore, Mother.
>	Take this peace offering,
>	breaking the chain of murders.

CLYTEMNESTRA
    And the tomb will be empty
    of your screams?

ELECTRA
    To make room for
    redeeming silence.

ORESTES
    I'll relinquish my knife.

CLYTEMNESTRA
    This is your only knife?

ORESTES
    It was a gift of my father,
    loot from the rubble of homes.
    Here, in the tomb of Agamemnon,
    I renounce the throne of blood,
    I denounce the throne of terror.

CLYTEMNESTRA
    I see no thrones.
    You're an isolated beast,
    an assassin of order.
    You're mentally ill,
    wanting a world
    all different. That's ill,
    face it. Get away,
    before you hurt yourself badly.
    Electra, save your brother,
    ranting in our house of madness.

ELECTRA
    I'll stand beside him.

CLYTEMNESTRA
Did I hurt you so much,
does this life so overwhelm you,
are you so inept, that you flee
to dreams and a quick death
given to dreaming?
Yes, for your protection,
my son, put down the knife.
Put it at my feet, yes,
make the ceremony.

CHORUS
We were always promised
this return. But
the earth does not tremble.
It rolls in a vacuum.
All we can say is
our minds are manipulated.
If this is the day of peace,
I'm here finally to know it.

ORESTES kneels at CLYTEMNESTRA'S feet.

ORESTES
We can rule together.
My destiny is
to make peace
with you, mother.

ORESTES puts the knife at her feet.
CLYTEMNESTRA stabs him in the neck with her knife.
ORESTES falls dead.

CLYTEMNESTRA
It takes more than a gesture
even from Orestes
to break the iron chain.

CHORUS
>Quick to die!
>A fool in a hurry!
>Isolated!

ELECTRA
>Useless!
>We don't need martyrs!
>For one minute
>we all had peace.

CLYTEMNESTRA
>Only the dead know peace.

ELECTRA
>It's madness, stop!

CLYTEMNESTRA
>I'll have no more of your
>screaming witness.
>Won't you join me
>in tears? Won't you rejoice?
>We're free of that terror.
>Won't you ever comfort me?

ELECTRA
>What was purged in
>this blood ritual
>of god-shaming sacrifice?
>May the spectacle of
>sacrifice satisfy
>the guilts and thrills
>of barbaric rites
>and bring the gods among us
>so we can be cleansed of
>the blood curses of our
>war ancestors.

ELECTRA goes to the body of ORESTES.
CLYTEMNESTRA stabs her.
ELECTRA falls dead.

> CLYTEMNESTRA
> This is the sacrifice,
> appropriate to the gods,
> that will call up the Furies.
>
> CHORUS
> You killed your children!
>
> CLYTEMNESTRA
> It was the enemies and
> the fates of the age
> doomed to self-destroy
> that killed them.
>
> CHORUS
> The power and the structure of power
> of the war-murder house of the war-king
> Atreus is dead. Agamemnon is dead.
> You must give up war power.
>
> CLYTEMNESTRA
> What is there to find,
> that means redemption? Don't we know
> already there's no source
> that will cleanse,
> only the cycle,
> never broken, still tragic,
> now dooming the race?

CHORUS goes to the dead bodies.

CHORUS
> Weight, heavy matter,
> called into language,
> closed into circles of hell,
> the dizzy meaning nothing,
> outcries for redemption,
> mass of the ancients, sacrifice,
> all sacred and strange,
> the words enduring,
> the gods enduring in words
> after their deaths to mean
> only pleasure: mysteries
> of the resurrection,
> the truth of the faith threatened.

CLYTEMNESTRA kills CHORUS.

CLYTEMNESTRA
> Dreamers! This is the age of
> final solutions. I have my rights,
> my power, my visions, my faith,
> my anger. I am the stronger.
> I have the will. I'll rule
> the earth in it eternal image.

CLYTEMNESTRA steps forward to pray.

> Lost goddess of grains
> and of justice, you, always mourning
> for your daughter gone to hell!
> Hecate! Hell's damn mother,
> goddess of witches!
> End my human being, make me
> the earth, angry and abused,
> spinning the fate of her scornful
> children, the restless, indifferent humans!

The earth groans in its spinning.
Dizzy, the seas slosh.
Nations take hold on the grinning
death head turning
in curved space, beginning
the end with sterile machines.

Now fear
the monumental
living rage of the Furies.
The Furies were queens of
the earth before the gods.
Blocked from this world,
their soul is the law: guilt!
They screech like bats at
the three-faced altar.
Their tongue is wrath.
Blood mumbles from their mouths.
They open out of hell
in vengeance, the Furies!

CLYTEMNESTRA exits.

The End

Lincoln in Queens

LINCOLN IN QUEENS

was first presented as a poetry reading with slides by William Considine at Solidaridad Humana on June 12, 1988, in a theater festival curated by Nina Zivancevic and Carlo Stephanos. The reading was later presented at Dixon Place and The Knitting Factory, all in downtown Manhattan.

A video with music by Gerry Hemingway was produced in January 1990 by Leigh Block and William Considine, using public access facilities at Station QPTV, Queens, of Time Warner Cable, and by audio producer Gerry Hemingway, using his studio.
Consulting producer, Jane Polisar. Artwork by Deborah Gans and photographs by William Considine.

The video appeared on cable television in Manhattan and Queens, and in the Videotech series at The Knitting Factory.

It is now available online, and can be found at:
https://www.youtube.com/watch?v=RvD2qJ9oshE

The audio track is on the CD, An Early Spring, from Fast Speaking Music.

LINCOLN IN QUEENS

Lincoln in Queens
is a tale.
This tale has seven
segments, called:

Iron
Unemployed
A Vision
Depression
Journey
The Furies
Offering

IRON

Both my grandfathers worked in the mills.
    Steelworkers.
My father was an unemployed
    steelworker when I was born.

The clangor and night fires of the vast
old mills along the rivers
swore to me in fearful curses
that the earth is iron and poor.
Steel mills burned the earth in my eyes.
Long trains loaded with coal or slag made my home
on a hill over the mill. Orange smoke from blast
furnaces billowed above Steel Valley.
Polluted rivers ran yellow and sluggish.
Men ate their earnings from a lunchbox.

    I am of the race of iron,
        still living in the Iron Age.
    Do I have to work at a blast furnace,
        do I have to make steel
    in a big, barn-like foundry
        between railroad tracks and the river?

The oldest poems that survive
condemn the race of iron
    to work and waste.

    "Our hearts are owned forever by war
    and the war debts of our fathers,"
        chanted the savages.
    "The people of iron destroy.
        We tear and burn the earth."

So we dreamed our fate into development.
    Or so the first poems say.
The author of "The Birth of Gods" says that
in his second song, "The Work Day."
I don't believe it. I think it's primitive.

In World War Two, my father blew up
ships on the huge moon
reflected on the Pacific Ocean.
He was a bombardier, in a black-painted
night raider, a Navy plane with pontoons.
They hid by day in bays of New Guinea.
After the war, he got a job in the mill,
but the work was dirty and hot,
with many lay-offs.
                       My father left the mill.
He got a job with the Fire Department.
He drove a red fire truck into danger.
He drove the pump truck at Number Four Station.

    I inherit fire-fighting too
    as my job in Iron City.
            It's a strenuous confusion.
The Iron Age rages with furnace fires.

UNEMPLOYED

My job is the most evil ever,
according to Plato. I write poems
about politics, not
from logic but from inspiration.
I excite myself and spurt disruptive
fantasies all over the social fabric,
in danger to the state and order.
But here's the irony,
iron-ee, iron I, the eye run of insight:
I dream of hidden logic.
I speak of ancient things, because
I search them for inspiration.
They are the wild wine I share with you.
 I violate another of Plato's rules
for Western Civilization: I should not know
so goddamn much about the rules.
I am of the race of iron. In a republic,
we must be taught with myths to do the work.
We must believe we were born in the earth
to work with dirt. We should only hear
about daylight from people of gold.
I have no gold in my nature, just red dirt.
With a resume like that, I was of course
out of work, like my father at my birth.

I was at the time of this story living
near a river and the ruins of factories,
               in Queens.
I was an unemployed lecturer in law.
I lived on unemployment benefits.
Each Thursday I reported to the state
on my efforts to find a new job.

One day in August I walked
to the State Office Building through the bleak,
hot, shadeless sameness of industrial Queens.
    I had to watch out for thundering big trucks,
    full of demolished debris.

                          I thought about
        money, jobs, women, big trucks, dramatic
        poetry, the landscape, the great city,
        my unhappy childhood, love, abandonment,
        the arms race and the worldwide crisis
        of production.

 What I resolved was this:
I would keep writing tragic plays, but
I would not get hit by a truck,
get to the unemployment office safely,
get a job, find a woman,
and fall in love even unwisely,
but as soon as possible.

A VISION

I was on my way to sign for my last
unemployment check.
I walked past auto body shops, past car wrecks
dumped on sidewalks outside open garages.
I walked by the ornate old courthouse
and onto a traffic island
named for a corporal killed in a war.
On that island of concrete in the streets
beyond the courthouse stood a man,
dressed all in black old clothes in the sun.
He was tall, lean and stooped. He stared at me.

I thought he was homeless and needed money.
He pointed at me and spoke:

> "You have obeyed the gods
> too long for our love.
> Now you must be punished
> with our last commandment:
>   Make peace!"

I stopped, astounded, for this man
had recited very well
verses from my play, "Electra."
He had played Apollo in a vision!
I turned about; no one else was around,
no one staring at this chanting man.
Still pointing, he went on:

> "You must set off at once
>   into impassable solitude
>   to find the Furies."

"I am the master of Furies," I snapped
at this insolent stranger. He snapped back:

    "The Furies will haunt you"

"Who are you?" I cried,
suddenly scared of the Furies.
    He just looked back at me.
He looked like Lincoln, but couldn't be,
    not back from the dead in Queens.
Yes, he was Abe Lincoln! The Emancipator.
He spoke softly, with quiet authority.

    "I abolished slavery through war.
        You must begin to abolish war.
    War is no more natural than slavery.
        The chain of war was dug from the earth
        by slaves, and it is made of iron.
    It's time to shut down the iron age
        and demolish a lot of useless things,
            like war!"

I was astonished by this vision
    and his vision of peace.
"How?"

        "You must find the Furies!
    Alecto, Megaera, Tisiphone!
    The female Furies ruled before the gods.
        They are forgotten and angry.
        They still feed our brain stems.
    The law of the Furies is guilt.
    The justice of Furies is terror.

"If we can free and appease the Furies,
the super spell on our minds will break.

> The war state will crumble.
> There will be good
> new jobs in a free spirit of work.

"And you must find the Furies."

"But ... the Furies are un-American,"
I cried. "They're archaic female powers.
They're ancient Greek ...
They're no way to communicate today.
No one will understand me when I talk
about Furies. They're like witches.
They're not the faith of Lincoln."

Lincoln spoke of God like a lost lover:

> "I lived in faith in the old-fashioned fable
>   of suffering and moral endurance.
> We purged the blood-curse on our nation:
>   slavery! Now you can escape
>   the iron shackles of war,
>   the fable of blood atonement,
>   the faith of Furies.
> Your hope is in creation.
>   I've given you a job!
>   Prophecy, abolish war!"

Lincoln turned away and entered
a grimy garage where men looked back at me
    with anger at my staring.
I called, "President Lincoln! Wait!
    Please, tell me a joke!"

Lincoln came out of the dark garage
where a radio blared. He laughed.
I was glad to see him smile, finally.

> "You know how long a person's legs must be,"
> he said. "Long enough to reach the ground.
> But how long must a person's arms reach?"

"Far enough to touch the stars," I said at once.

> "Far enough to touch the people you love."
> Lincoln turned and walked into the garage,
> and men pulled down the clamoring, blank
> metal door that gleamed silver in the harsh sun.

DEPRESSION

I told my girlfriend
Lincoln himself ordered me
to set off at once into impassable
solitude. Right away she left me.
My job was impossible.
Finding Furies could not end war.
Furies were metaphors, myths.
They were obsolete myths,
no contemporary resonance.
I was trapped in poetic language,
struggling to speak in politics.
I was sure to self-destruct on this mission.
But I searched for the Furies in old books, in
troubled sleep and on my walls and ceiling.
My productivity declined.
I stole my own thoughts from others.
I went out to hear poets
in readings in cafes and bars in slums.
I was out of place in public and retreated.
I lay heart-sick in the fetal position.

I was totally laid-off.
My depression deepened in a worldwide
structure of depression. The spirit of
ego had seized the meaning of work, and
the spirit of work had nothing to do.
I was broke, broken, guilty,
obeying the dead in a futile endeavor
to raise the dawn.

I applied for a job as a judge.
I put on a suit and rode the subway,
as if I had a job. I was happy there.
I realized, I was already in love unwisely.
There was no rush to find love.
She wrote me a letter, just to say
good-bye again. I could read it over and over.
Love would be even better after the iron age.

JOURNEY

Out of a desk drawer, I finally pulled
my credit card, my MasterCard!
I'd saved it from better days
as my last resource till I found work.
I stared at the plastic key to
$1,000 credit!

        I leapt in search of the Furies.
I bought a plane ticket to New Mexico
        and flew off at once.
I rented a car with my charge card
and drove into the mountains
        of the blood of Christ,
up a winding road beside chasms,
from scrub pine and silvery sage shrubs
through pine forest to the hidden summit
        of Los Alamos.
                I searched
where men created the atom bomb,
        to find the Furies and unlock creation.

Los Alamos was bland on a bright,
steam-shovel leveled mountain top,
planted with grass and suburban structures
around huge, guarded hangars and buildings
for nuclear weapons research.
I drove round and round in a rented car,
watched by guards at the many gates,
with nowhere to stop but a small museum
and a duck pond where the ice house had been,
        where they built the bomb.
I found no inspiration in the vast enterprise.
The place made me numb. I had to leave.
I'd thrown away a thousand dollars
        I didn't have.

Driving down the mountain, at its base,
in scrub pine and silvery sage shrubs,
I followed signs to cliff dwellings
of vanished Indians. The cliffs were white stone.
Alone, I climbed ladders up a cliff
and sat in a hollow looking south
to the white sands desert of Alamogordo.

          Alecto
                    Megaera
                              Tisiphone

Where are the Furies?
            Hags! Witches!
Old crones of the moon,
            withered ancients?
Or young girls from the dawn of humanity?
            Or my furious mother?
                        Dead ten years ...

The Furies chase the damned.
              Wasn't my mission to end war,
                        my trip to this cave,
                        a mad, haunted flight
                                    of the damned?

My furious mother
            sat in the cave beside me.
                        We looked at each other,
unable to reach each other,
            and we cried,
caught together in heavy chains of suicide.

THE FURIES

My mother had worked in a five-and-ten
after high school. Then she got married
to a young veteran who worked in the mill.
I learned words at her feet, learned to read
while she did the ironing
in hissing steam clouds.
She liked to get out, to go bowling
or, in her black dress, to a banquet
of the American Legion or the song club.
Her neck swelled, scaring us all.
Her thyroid pumped adrenaline too fast.
She saw too fiercely too much that made her
miserable, fearful, frantic to escape.
My parents had terrible fights for years.

In a confused and shameful divorce,
she gave up custody of her children.
She found work with a dentist,
but she had cancer and brutal surgery.
She stayed alive for years, on welfare,
chattering non-stop when I visited,
home from college or law school.
Her apartment was closed and stifling.
Her refrigerator held laundry and beer.
The closets held piles of pill bottles.
She left a note when she died.
Maybe she killed herself,
to end her solitary suffering.

Now she sat beside me in a hollow
in a white cliff below Los Alamos.
I said,

"I'm sorry
I've disturbed you in death.
    I often dream of you:
confused in my somber dream,
    baffled by death,
you shiver and sit down.
    You stay,
as if you are home
    in a new house, full of fear
you show as nervousness.
    You keep making jokes,
nervously.
    Taking your hand,
I talk you, elaborately, away.
    You take my hand
with fake good humor,
    to wander slowly out
of the place, as I let go.
    I'm still afraid to keep you.
Our loss of family life
    was brutal, but blameless,
I hope.
    I'm still mourning,
in my on-going
    difficulties in love."

She said,
"You know you left me alone
when I was sick,
when I wanted to live with you."

I said,
    "I had to make my own way.
    You wanted me to stay in school."

She said,

"But then you threw away
your chances to make good.

Now you sit in a cave as a failure.
Now making your way
is not so very important.
I can live with you now, please."

I held out my hand to her.
She took my hand and got up.
We looked at each other
as if for the last time,
like the last time we saw each other.
I said, "Yes, we do live together."
We embraced, and
                I stood alone in a cave
looking south to the white sands
of Alamogordo.

OFFERING

I returned to New York
and took work as an office temp,
humiliated by clerical work
        in a Wall Street law firm.

        I reflected on my search for the Furies:
        spinning circles,
                the driven and mad,
        pursuing ourselves.
Finding my mother as my Furies
seemed so much a cop-out
        on politics, more failure.

                Then I knew that voice inside,
haunting my every move,
was the Furies.
        I'm at home with Furies.
The Furies press home doubts,
        sneering like children
repeating the scorn they heard in their parents.
        The Furies accuse
        and I answer by shaping peace
in fragments
        I must make to be complete.

"Will you make offerings to lost spirits?"
the Furies ask with big, skeptical eyes.

So, I offer this work to lost spirits.
May we make peace as we find them.

conceptual framework

The Furies is an attack in dramatic verse on mythic sources of war and the tragic cycle. What starts in jest and hope becomes tragic and then quite personal. The source work for the cycle is Aeschylus' *Oresteia*, radically revised.

Prologue: Prehistory sets the stage in theater and theory, words from the same root. I returned to the foundational story of Solon in the full-length poetic drama, *Women's Mysteries*.

Agamemnon, King of Cars is a comic goat song; Iphigenia refuses to be sacrificed, Odysseus returns from the underworld to plead for peace, and the chorus decline to go to war. It has roots in street theater, with a nod to a performance I saw of the San Francisco Mime Troupe, though this was never a street piece. The jokes are now untimely, but more serious concerns remain constant.

Electra turns the foretold stories on their head, as Electra and Orestes refuse their parts, leading to new tragedy. Sophocles' *Electra*, with its relentless pacing, was a model for my smaller effort.

Lincoln in Queens is a tale in which Lincoln commands a contemporary poet to go in search of the fabled Furies, to free them and abolish war. It's a tale in seven segments - *Iron, Unemployed, A Vision, Depression, Journey, The Furies,* and *Offering* - ranging from the Rustbelt and lingering wounds of a global war through personal and global depression to a final vision at the white sands of Alamogordo. Its offering must serve humbly in place of *The Eumenides*.

These pieces, produced separately in small venues over a period of years, are brought together here for the first time as a unified series.

I wish to express here my gratitude to the many people who gave of their time so generously to participate in these uncompensated theater productions. The actors, directors and other artists are named in the respective credits. Many were good friends and all were dedicated artists. Thank you.

- William Considine, 2017

william considine :
a life as poetics and practice

I was born in McKeesport, Pennsylvania, a steel mill city on the Monongahela River near Pittsburgh. My father was a fireman and did plumbing on the side. My mother cared for three boys and later worked as a dental assistant. I first worked as a helper for my father, later as a caddie and soda jerk.

Love of theater may have come first from middle school experiences writing and staging satirical skits. I remember TV quiz show scandals as one of my comic targets. Perhaps the first poem I engaged, also in middle school, was Whitman's "O Captain! My Captain!" I read Aeschylus' *Oresteia* on my own one summer while still working for my father, in a torn-cover paperback I'd bought for a quarter. I read a lot, already dreaming of writing. A great source for reading was the Carnegie Free Library. In high school, I was on the school newspaper and in speech club and on the debate team, further signs of my continuing interest in writing and speaking.

I attended Stanford University on a scholarship and work-study. I majored in political science, with a lot of economics and history. I had put aside creative writing as an unrealistic goal and was consumed by public events and their causes. I worked as a student guide, giving tours of campus and assisting visitors to an observation platform. I graduated "With Great Distinction" in 1970.

At Stanford, Diane Middlebrook first encouraged me to write poetry. I took her Introduction to Poetry course as a senior and loved it. She arranged further study for me in my last term. I first studied writing poetry with Elizabeth Bishop, in her seminar at Harvard in 1972. I was in the law school and could cross-register for one course.

I graduated cum laude from Harvard Law School in 1973. Initially, I worked full-time as an attorney and wrote in the evenings. Then, I served in part-time positions for several years, including teaching law as an adjunct at Pace Law School and conducting hearings as an administrative law judge, while devoting myself largely to writing.

I was a member of the New York Shakespeare Festival's Playwrights Unit at the Public Theater, coordinated by Ed Bullins, from 1977 through 1980. There, I developed scenes and had staged readings of four of my plays

Agamemnon, King of Cars, a verse play, was my first production, in a festival at Theater for the New City in June 1982.

I soon was active in the East Village poetry world, with numerous public readings. The No Se No social club was an especially important place in my development, in the summer of 1983, as an open, creative community. My poems appeared over the next several years in local publications including *Downtown, Red Tape, Cover, New Observations, Pan Arts* and *The National Poetry Journal of the Lower East Side*.

My verse play, *Electra*, was performed in an arts exhibition at the Brooklyn Army Terminal in October 1983. A video by Franz Vila of the play in performance appeared in early 1984, my first video.

I made poetry videos during the mid-1980's with Edmond Chibeau and Mitch Corber. In 1990, I co-produced with Leigh Block a video of my poem, *Lincoln in Queens*, with music by jazz artist Gerry Hemingway. It won an award for video produced on public access facilities.

I participated in the annual Poets Theater Festival of the St. Marks Poetry Project, coordinated by Bob Holman, in 1988-90 at the Theater at 2nd and 10th and at LaMama. There, I also developed scenes of what became a full-length poetic drama, *Women's Mysteries*.

I then had a lengthy hiatus as a writer, to focus on full-time responsibilities with work and family. I no longer found it possible to change from work to writing in the course of a day or weeks, or to follow up on any writing that I did. I've had a career of some forty years in the law, primarily in local government and with a non-profit organization for dispute resolution.

While still working, I returned to poetry in 2011. My first concern was to digitize old creative work before the videotapes deteriorated too far. From that impulse came renewed interest in writing again. I took numerous writers workshops, particularly at the St. Marks Poetry Project, to sustain continued focus on writing, educate myself on what I had missed, meet poets and participate again in an active community. I was fortunate in having access to outstanding, often much younger poets as workshop teachers over several years.

In 2013, The Operating System (then known as Exit Strata) published a chapbook of some of my older poems, *Strange Coherence*. That same year, Fast Speaking Music issued a CD of my poems with music, *An Early Spring*. The Medicine Show Theatre presented a staged reading of *Women's Mysteries* in 2015.

I retired from practicing law in May 2016. I live in Brooklyn with Careen Shannon, my wife. My daughter Emma also lives in New York City and my step-daughter Rachel in San Francisco.

I am happy that these related plays (and poem) are being published together now as The Furies, and grateful to publisher and guide, Lynne DeSilva-Johnson.

𝔞𝔯𝔠𝔥𝔦𝔳𝔞𝔩 𝔭𝔥𝔬𝔱𝔬𝔰 𝔞𝔫𝔡 𝔡𝔬𝔠𝔲𝔪𝔢𝔫𝔱𝔰
𝔣𝔯𝔬𝔪 𝔬𝔯𝔦𝔤𝔦𝔫𝔞𝔩 𝔭𝔯𝔬𝔡𝔲𝔠𝔱𝔦𝔬𝔫𝔰

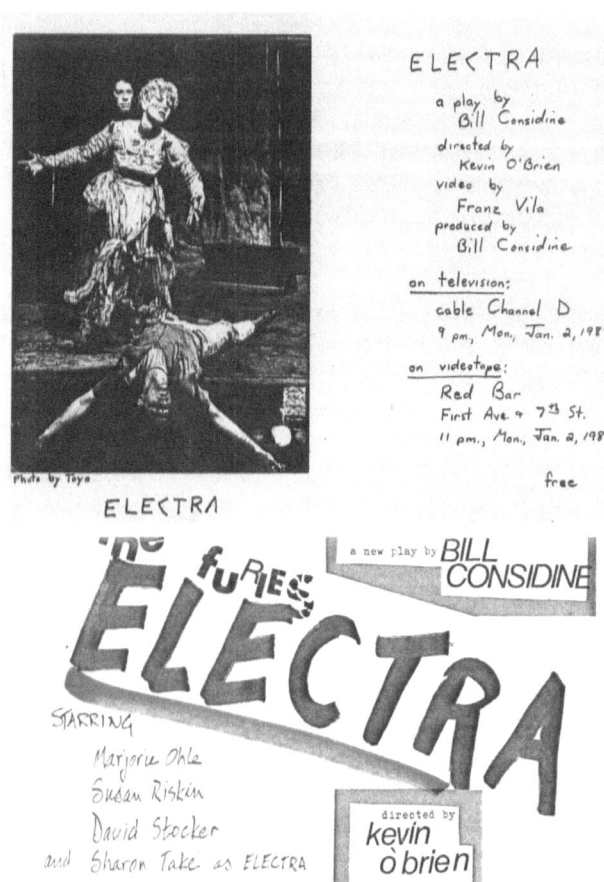

ELECTRA @ Brooklyn Army Terminal, 1983

Sharon Take as Electra
(photo: Toyo Tsuchiya)

Sharon Take, L; Susan Riskin as Clytemnestra, R; painted set designed by John Shaw, stage furniture by Frank Shifreen (photo: Toyo Tsuchiya)

THE FURIES: ELECTRA

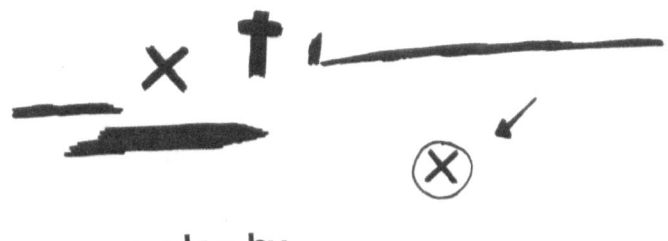

a play by

Bill Considine

October 22 and 23

TERMINAL

L-R: Sharon Take, Marjorie Ohle, Bill Considine, onsite.

Sharon Take, L; David Stocker as Orestes, R;
(photo: Toyo Tsuchiya)

Electra and Orestes (Take and Stocker), both pages.
(photos: Toyo Tsuchiya)

Top: L-R: Marjorie Ohle as Chorus, Sharon Take, Susan Riskin

Top: Cast and crew photo from ELECTRA, with (standing L-R) Sharon Take, David Stocker, Michael Curtin, Marjorie Ohle, Susan Riskin, director Kevin O'Brien, Dave Lancet and (in front) playwright Bill Considine. Right: in performance at the Brooklyn Army Terminal, David Stocker enters along the tracks as Messenger. Below (clockwise from left): photographer Toyo Tsuchiya at an exhibit of his photos with Considine, Stocker, and Take.

Photos for LINCOLN IN QUEENS, 1988-90. All photos, Bill Considine unless otherwise noted.

Above: bronze sculpture of Abraham Lincoln, Union Square Park, NY. Henry Kirke Brown, 1870.

Above: Overgrown abandoned freight loading dock, Long Island City, Queens.

Below: New York State Unemployment Office, Queens Plaza, Queens, New York.

Above: Long Island City, Queens

Below: the author, at blast furnaces of U.S. Steel's National Works, McKeesport, PA (photographed by his father, William Considine)

Both Photos: Steel Plant, Duquesne Works, Duquesne, PA

Above: Set Maquette by Deborah Gans, 1986

Below: Blast Furnaces, U.S. Steel's National Works, McKeesport, PA

Above: Steel Plant at McKeesport/Duquesne Works, PA

Below: Empire City Iron Works Signage, Long Island City

Steel Plants at McKeesport/Duquesne Works, PA

Abandoned industrial loading pier, Long Island City, Queens

Above: Chain / fences, Long Island City,

Below: Composite image by Deborah Gans, 1986, adapted for Lincoln in Queens

Above: Loading Dock composite image by Deborah Gans, 1986, adapted for Lincoln in Queens

Below: Metal door detail, LIC, Queens, NY

Long Island City with Manhattan seen in the background, New York City, 1988

photo: Tom Warren

poetics, playwrighting and process :
an interview with bill considine and lynne desilva-johnson

Greetings comrade!
Thank you for talking to us about your process today!

I appreciate the opportunity - and the challenge of addressing some questions I've never had to answer, even to myself!

Can you introduce yourself, in a way that you would choose?

I'm a retired lawyer in my late 60's. I come from a working-class background in a declining Rust Belt mill town, but that was a long time ago. I had the benefit of a terrific education. I chose to live in a vibrant, creative center and participate. I always wanted to write, and over time I've written a lot.

Why are you a poet/writer/artist/playwright?

I wanted to express myself, and to play with language. I enjoy writing. Making a poem is one of life's great joys.

When did you decide you were a poet/writer/artist/playwright (and/or: do you feel comfortable calling yourself a poet/writer/artist/playwright, what other titles or affiliations do you prefer/feel are more accurate)?

I wanted to write since I was quite young. I read voraciously. I was very interested in politics and history, as well as literature. I decided, before college, that it was unrealistic to expect to live as a writer, and I focused in college on social studies. By the time I was a senior, I was taking courses in philosophy and then, in my last terms, in poetry. Law school largely bored me, and I wrote a play. My first wife encouraged me. She was an actress. She earned a masters degree in theater and performed, even on Broadway. I wrote several plays, in the evenings and weekends, while working as a young lawyer in New York over a period of years. Then I felt strongly that I needed to devote myself to my art. Years of discouragement in theater ultimately brought me back to only my own resources. I could not expect anyone to actualize my plays. What I wrote and spoke aloud myself was all I could rely on. With that realization, I was a poet.

What do you see as the relationship between being a "poet" and being a "playwright?" How does that work in your practice?

Well, they're two different communities or worlds. There are relatively few people active in both worlds. That separation of the two arts and communities did not work in my favor.

I've been returning recently to playwriting. In part, this is because I have always been drawn to longer or larger forms, and to multiple voices instead of only the lyric self.

What's a "poet," anyway? What do you see as your cultural and social role (in the literary / artistic / creative community and beyond)?

A poet is a worker in language, making words fresh and honest and exploratory. But that is too laborious: A poet plays with language, because words define our world, and because it's fun.

In the literary community, I am, I hope, attentive to others' work and encouraging. Poets help sustain each other.

Talk about the process or instinct to move these plays as independent entities into a body of work. How and why did this happen? Have you had this intention for a while? What encouraged and/or confounded this (or a book, in general) coming together? Was it a struggle?

These plays developed organically over time from my impulse to write verse plays, to combine poetry and theater, which is a great tradition. I also had the impulse to de-construct, to re-write certain governing myths. *Agamemnon, King of Cars* was a comedy, so then I wanted to write a tragedy too, and *Electra* came from that. It took some years to find the third piece, an equivalent to *The Eumenides* in the ancient trilogy. In those years, I made poems and videos. *Lincoln in Queens* finally emerged.

I then wrote another Greek play, a full-length verse drama based on a story in Plutarch, *Women's Mysteries*. It too is about the drive to war in myth and history. I see that play as a second piece in a larger-scale trilogy, with *The Furies* as the first piece. I've drafted some of a third piece, too.

Prologue: Prehistory was an early exploration toward *Women's Mysteries*. It belongs with these plays in *The Furies*, because it is an entry point into the force field of mythic origins, and it helps tie the larger structure together. It is echoed by a prologue in *Women's Mysteries*.

So, in my own mind, I had a relatively large-scale, unified set of plays, but this was utterly unknown. When you asked what I would want to publish now, my first and only thought was to bring these separately produced plays together as the whole that I intended.

When you were writing these plays, (or in general, when you write plays or other work to be performed), did you imagine them also being read? Have you ever written plays or used writing structures from theater to produce work that was intended primarily for the page?

Yes, I also imagine them being read. There are dramatic shapes to some of my poems. *Lincoln in Queens* after all is a poem, but I've included it in a volume of plays, where it belongs.

It's a very interesting phenomena, I think, the publishing and reading of plays -- unique amongst performance media as one that lives quite commonly in our experience both on the stage and the page, in life and in the classroom.

Do you think that the publishing of plays needs to treat the medium differently than it does other poetry, prose, or text? Talk a little more about your relationship to plays on the page versus on the stage, both as reader and producer / maker / writer.

I like to see the continuous flow of verse down the page, so I name the speakers at the left margin, not in the center. It shows the play as a poem more clearly on the page. I have always liked reading plays, because they move so briskly. Poetry's concision and sharpness serve drama well.

I have participated in many poetry readings, and the oral aspect of poetry is key for me, which is an understanding that lends itself to theater.

What formal structures or other constrictive practices (if any) do you use in the creation of your work, whether poetics or drama? Have certain teachers or instructive environments, or readings/writings/work of other creative people informed the way you work/write?

Using the medium of verse drama and using classical allusion and de-construction are themselves significant constraints. Otherwise, I have not used constraints as a creative practice.

What has most informed me in playwriting has been rehearsals. Seeing that something doesn't work and cutting or replacing it, or seeing that something more is needed, emerges from the rehearsal process.

Numerous poetry workshops over the past several years have informed me as a writer, and I am grateful to instructors and colleagues. That poets persist is among the most important lessons. One device so many recommend, that has not worked well for me yet, is to do free writing daily. I hate what I write down when I don't feel inspired. It is painful to put down just anything. Long ago, I kept a journal for several years. I felt the journal replaced creative writing.

Maybe I will acquire the habit of daily free writing yet! Any day now...

Speaking of monikers, what does your title represent? How was it generated? Talk about the way you titled the book, and how your process of naming (individual pieces, sections, etc) influences you and/or colors your work specifically.

Nearness of unseen Furies figures in both *Electra* and *Lincoln in Queens*. Clytemnestra calls down the Furies at the end of *Electra*. Besides being the book title, "The Furies" is also a segment title in *Lincoln in Queens*, which relates an impelled search for the Furies.

The Furies are problematic, because they're powerful but negative female figures identified with darkness, guilt and fear. I maximized that dark female aspect by portraying Clytemnestra as an onstage killer. When I put on *Electra*, I experimented with called it *The Furies: Electra*, as seen in a flyer for the play and in the name of the video. That title also meant to convey the fury of war, the urgency of war state resistance, and the rapid pace of the play.

In the larger structure, the transition from mythic Furies to the mother in *Lincoln in Queens* and to the women in *Women's Mysteries* is an important progression. The work overall seeks an escape from the tyranny of old myths and misperceptions.

What does this particular work represent to you as indicative of your method/creative practice, history, mission/intentions/hopes/plans?

This book represents a core of my creative work over the years, the attempt to integrate poetry and drama. It also shows a core focus on the power of the war state and aggressive, siege mentality. I looked to the Greeks partly to escape the more pertinent and overwhelming model for verse plays in English, Shakespeare. I thought that I would learn from Greek models and move on to other settings and eras. That didn't happen. Time is shorter now.

I want to complete the larger-scale trilogy that I discussed above. Beyond that, I hope to move in a new direction. That may be another verse drama or an echo of it. I may also get more prosaic. As a lawyer, I wrote a lot of prose. It flows more readily. I have a couple short prose pieces being published in journals this Fall.

What does this book DO (as much as what it says or contains)?

This book is an artifact of ambitions and dreams. I hope it may inspire others.

What would be the best possible outcome for this book? What might it do in the world, and how will its presence as an object facilitate your creative role in your community and beyond? What are your hopes for this book, and for your practice?

The best outcome would be for the book to inspire readings and productions, and for those productions to speak for the necessary but difficult process of finding and making peace.

Let's talk a little bit about the role of poetics and creative community in social activism, in particular in what I call "Civil Rights 2.0," which has remained immediately present all around us in the time leading up to this series' publication. I'd be curious to hear some thoughts on the challenges we face in speaking and publishing across lines of race, age, privilege, social/cultural background, and sexuality within the community, vs. the dangers of remaining and producing in isolated "silos."

These are big challenges, and our nation has suddenly taken a large step backwards. I think the keys are respect for others and openness to recognizing privilege in ourselves and in our assumptions about others.

Is there anything else we should have asked, or that you want to share?

Thank you for this opportunity!

WHY PRINT / DOCUMENT?

The Operating System uses the language "print document" to differentiate from the book-object as part of our mission to distinguish the act of documentation-in-book-FORM from the act of publishing as a backwards facing replication of the book's agentive *role* as it may have appeared the last several centuries of its history. Ultimately, I approach the book as TECHNOLOGY: one of a variety of printed documents (in this case bound) that humans have invented and in turn used to archive and disseminate ideas, beliefs, stories, and other evidence of production.

Ownership and use of printing presses and access to (or restriction of printed materials) has long been a site of struggle, related in many ways to revolutionary activity and the fight for civil rights and free speech all over the world. While (in many countries) the contemporary quotidian landscape has indeed drastically shifted in its access to platforms for sharing information and in the widespread ability to "publish" digitally, even with extremely limited resources, the importance of publication on physical media has not diminished. In fact, this may be the most critical time in recent history for activist groups, artists, and others to insist upon learning, establishing, and encouraging personal and community documentation practices. Hear me out.

With The OS's print endeavors I wanted to open up a conversation about this: the ultimately radical, transgressive act of creating PRINT /DOCUMENTATION in the digital age. It's a question of the archive, and of history: who gets to tell the story, and what evidence of our life, our behaviors, our experiences are we leaving behind? We can know little to nothing about the future into which we're leaving an unprecedentedly digital document trail – but we can be assured that publications, government agencies, museums, schools, and other institutional powers that be will continue to leave BOTH a digital and print version of their production for the official record. Will we?

As a (rogue) anthropologist and long time academic, I can easily pull up many accounts about how lives, behaviors, experiences – how THE STORY of a time or place – was pieced together using the deep study of correspondence, notebooks, and other physical documents which are no longer the norm in many lives and practices. As we move our creative behaviors towards digital note taking, and even audio and video, what can we predict about future technology that is in any way assuring that our stories will be accurately told – or told at all? How will we leave these things for the record?

In these documents we say:
WE WERE HERE, WE EXISTED, WE HAVE A DIFFERENT STORY

- Lynne DeSilva-Johnson, Founder/Managing Editor,
THE OPERATING SYSTEM, Brooklyn NY 2017

TITLES IN THE PRINT: DOCUMENT COLLECTION

An Absence So Great and Spontaneous It Is Evidence of Light - Anne Gorrick [2018]
Chlorosis - Michael Flatt and Derrick Mund [2018]
Sussuros a Mi Padre - Erick Sáenz [2018]
Sharing Plastic - Blake Nemec [2018]
The Book of Sounds - Mehdi Navid (trans. Tina Rahimi) [2018]
Abandoners - Lesley Ann Wheeler [2018]
Jazzercise is a Language - Gabriel Ojeda-Sague [2018]
Death is a Festival - Anis Shivani [2018]
Return Trip / Viaje Al Regreso; Dual Language Edition -
Israel Dominguez,(trans. Margaret Randall) [2018]
Born Again - Ivy Johnson [2018]
Singing for Nothing - Wally Swist [2018]

One More Revolution - Andrea Mazzariello [2017]
Fugue State Beach - Filip Marinovich [2017]
Lost City Hydrothermal Field - Peter Milne Greiner [2017]
The Book of Everyday Instruction - Chloe Bass [2017]
In Corpore Sano : Creative Practice and the Challenged Body
[Anthology, 2017] Lynne DeSilva-Johnson and Jay Besemer, co-editors
Love, Robot - Margaret Rhee[2017]
The Furies - William Considine [2017]
Nothing Is Wasted - Shabnam Piryaei [2017]
Mary of the Seas - Joanna C. Valente [2017]
Secret-Telling Bones - Jessica Tyner Mehta [2017]
CHAPBOOK SERIES 2017 : INCANTATIONS
featuring original cover art by Barbara Byers
sp. - Susan Charkes; Radio Poems - Jeffrey Cyphers Wright; Fixing a Witch/Hexing the Stitch - Jacklyn Janeksela; cosmos a personal voyage by carl sagan ann druyan steven sotor and me - Connie Mae Oliver
Flower World Variations, Expanded Edition/Reissue - Jerome Rothenberg and Harold Cohen [2017]
Island - Tom Haviv [2017]
What the Werewolf Told Them / Lo Que Les Dijo El Licantropo -
Chely Lima (trans. Margaret Randall) [2017]
The Color She Gave Gravity - Stephanie Heit [2017]
The Science of Things Familiar - Johnny Damm [Graphic Hybrid, 2017]
agon - Judith Goldman [2017]
To Have Been There Then / Estar Alli Entonces - Gregory Randall
(trans. Margaret Randall) [2017]

Instructions Within - Ashraf Fayadh [2016]
Arabic-English dual language edition; Mona Kareem, translator
Let it Die Hungry - Caits Meissner [2016]
A GUN SHOW - Adam Sliwinski and Lynne DeSilva-Johnson;
So Percussion in Performance with Ain Gordon and Emily Johnson [2016]
Everybody's Automat [2016] - Mark Gurarie
How to Survive the Coming Collapse of Civilization [2016] - Sparrow
CHAPBOOK SERIES 2016: OF SOUND MIND
*featuring the quilt drawings of Daphne Taylor
Improper Maps - Alex Crowley; While Listening - Alaina Ferris;
Chords - Peter Longofono; Any Seam or Needlework - Stanford Cheung

TEN FOUR - Poems, Translations, Variations [2015] - Jerome Rothenberg, Ariel Resnikoff, Mikhl Likht (w/ Stephen Ross)
MARILYN [2015] - Amanda Ngoho Reavey
CHAPBOOK SERIES 2015: OF SYSTEMS OF
*featuring original cover art by Emma Steinkraus
Cyclorama - Davy Knittle; The Sensitive Boy Slumber Party Manifesto
- Joseph Cuillier; Neptune Court - Anton Yakovlev; Schema - Anurak Saelow
SAY/MIRROR [2015; 2nd edition 2016] - JP HOWARD
Moons Of Jupiter/Tales From The Schminke Tub [plays, 2014] - Steve Danziger

CHAPBOOK SERIES 2014: BY HAND
Pull, A Ballad - Maryam Parhizkar; Can You See that Sound - Jeff Musillo
Executive Producer Chris Carter - Peter Milne Grenier;
Spooky Action at a Distance - Gregory Crosby;

CHAPBOOK SERIES 2013: WOODBLOCK
*featuring original prints from Kevin William Reed
Strange Coherence - Bill Considine; The Sword of Things - Tony Hoffman;
Talk About Man Proof - Lancelot Runge / John Kropa; An Admission as a Warning
Against the Value of Our Conclusions - Alexis Quinlan

DOC U MENT
/däkyəmənt/

First meant "instruction" or "evidence," whether written or not.

noun - a piece of written, printed, or electronic matter that provides information or evidence or that serves as an official record
verb - record (something) in written, photographic, or other form
synonyms - paper - deed - record - writing - act - instrument

[*Middle English, precept, from Old French, from Latin documentum, example, proof, from docre, to teach; see dek- in Indo-European roots.*]

Who is responsible for the manufacture of value?
Based on what supercilious ontology have we landed in a space where we vie against other creative people in vain pursuit of the fleeting credibilities of the scarcity economy, rather than freely collaborating and sharing openly with each other in ecstatic celebration of MAKING?

While we understand and acknowledge the economic pressures and fear-mongering that threatens to dominate and crush the creative impulse,
we also believe that **now more than ever**
we have the tools to relinquish agency via cooperative means,
fueled by the fires of the Open Source Movement.

Looking out across the invisible vistas of that rhizomatic parallel country
we can begin to see our community beyond constraints,
in the place where intention meets
resilient, proactive, collaborative organization.

Here is a document born of that belief, sown purely of imagination and will.
When we document we assert.
We print to make real, to reify our being there.
When we do so with mindful intention to address our process,
to open our work to others, to create beauty in words in space, to respect
and acknowledge the strength of the page we now hold physical,
a thing in our hand… we remind ourselves that, like Dorothy:
we had the power all along, my dears.

THE PRINT! DOCUMENT SERIES
is a project of
the trouble with bartleby
in collaboration with
the operating system

www.ingramcontent.com/pod-product-compliance
Lightning Source LLC
Chambersburg PA
CBHW021440080526
44588CB00009B/619